Who Are You Calling a Woolly Mammoth?

Prehistoric America

by Elizabeth Levy

Additional Material by J. R. Havlan

Illustrated by Daniel McFeeley

D0973131

SCHOLASTIC INC.
New York Toronto London Auckland Sydney
Mexico City New Delhi Hong Kong

Scholastic gratefully acknowledges the original inspiration of Terry Deary's *Horrible Histories* series, published by Scholastic Publications Ltd., London, U.K.

If you purchased this book without a cover, you should be aware that this book is stolen property. It was reported as "unsold and destroyed" to the publisher, and neither the author nor the publisher has received any payment for this "stripped book."

No part of this publication may be reproduced in whole or in part, or stored in a retrieval system, or transmitted in any form or by any means, electronic, mechanical, photocopying, recording, or otherwise, without written permission of the publisher. For information regarding permission, write to Scholastic Inc., Attention: Permissions Dept., 555 Broadway, New York, NY 10012.

0-590-12938-4
Cover illustration: Mick McGinty
Cover design and art direction: Ursula S. Albano
Interior design: Kevin Callahan / BNGO Books
Text copyright © 2000 by Elizabeth Levy
www.ElizabethLevy.com

Illustrations copyright © 2000 by Scholastic Inc.
All rights reserved. Published by Scholastic Inc.

SCHOLASTIC and associated logos are trademarks and/or registered trademarks of Scholastic Inc.

12 11 10 9 8 7 6 5 4 3 2   1 2 3 4 5/0
                                                       40

Printed in the U.S.A.
First Scholastic printing, September 2000

To Rabbi Joseph Fink, who taught me that rarely does anybody get more than a beautiful "sliver" of the whole truth and who also liked to end services in time for Friday-night wrestling, proving that great humanitarianism and wackiness can go hand in hand. — E. L.

Acknowledgments

First of all, thanks to Jean Feiwel, who was wacky and courageous enough to allow me to try putting my love of history and my love of humor together. To Sheila Keenan, who patiently saw this book through endless drafts and helped pull it all together well beyond the call of duty. Thanks also to Susan Jeffers Casel for her careful and thoughtful copy editing. To Ursula Albano for her patience and vision as art director. To Professor Terry Harrison of New York University, who helped as the scope of the project kept getting wider and wider. To Amy Berkower at Writers House, who had such faith in this project. To Paula Danziger and Robie Harris, two wonderful friends and writers who groaned at my puns. To Dr. Murray List, who put up with my own groans at the growing pains of this project.

Expert Reader: Jay Holmes, After-School Program Coordinator/Ecology Club Advisor, Education Department, American Museum of Natural History, New York, New York

What's So Funny?

History is usually a random, messy affair . . .
Mark Twain, *A Horse's Tail*

The one who tells the stories rules the world.
Hopi saying

Humor and history have a lot in common. They let everybody in on the joke about how funny, impossible, clever, misguided, smart, or silly humans can be and have always been. History and jokes can be horrible and wacky, often at the same time. Horrible comes from the Latin word *horree,* which means to bristle, to make your hairs stand on end. Wacky comes from the Old English word *thwack,* from the sound a stick would make smacking something or someone. So at the very least, the wacky and horrible parts of history will wake you up.

There's a saying that if you don't know your own history, you are condemned to repeat it. I say that if we can't laugh at ourselves, we're in even worse trouble. There are facts and jokes in this book that will make you laugh out loud, ones that will make you grin and groan, and ones that will make you squirm. Just check out the joke on the next page.

See what I mean, that *is* a disgusting joke below, but it's true. Dinosaurs did leave their droppings, some over a foot long, all over what is now the United States. Scientists even gave the dino dung a fancy name, coprolites. So while you're laughing at this and all the other jokes and cartoons in *Who Are You Calling a Woolly Mammoth?*, don't forget that the information here is real, at least as far as anybody knows. Just remember, historians keep learning and the ideas about what has really happened in the past sometimes change as often as most people change their underwear.

What's a foot long and hard as a rock?

Dinosaur droppings.

The Search for History's Lost Jokes

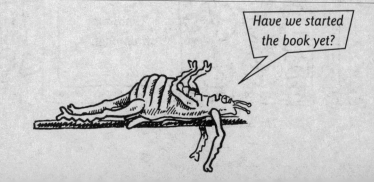

Have we started
the book yet?

Contents

Introduction

Some people think North American history began when Columbus sailed over in 1492 or when the first Vikings docked here around the year 1000, right around the time of the dreaded Y1K bug. Still others go further back and start counting when the first people appeared during America's last ice age, at least 12,500 years ago. But what about all the dinosaurs, mammoths, saber-toothed cats, and yes, even cockroaches, that crawled, lumbered, and stalked across North America before there *were* any people?

When I started researching *America's Horrible Histories*, I decided to go way, way back. All the way back to when North America broke apart from the world's supercontinent, Pangaea. All the way back to a time when incredible animals and prehistoric people wandered freely all over North America, across what is now Canada, the United States, Mexico, and down to Panama. All the way back to the unwritten, prehistoric story of American history, the one told in fossils, bones, and bugs in amber.

Speaking of bugs, what was one of the first land animals to leave its tiny footprints on American soil? The lowly cockroach! With its six hairy legs and two little hairs on its rear end to tell it if something is sneaking up from behind, this wily bug has survived 300 million years of history. (Who would have ever thought a hairy butt would come in handy?) They survived killer meteors and deadly ice ages. No ifs, ands, or but(t)s about it, cockroaches deserve the title, America's first settlers.

Lowly? This is a $500 suit!

But nobody, not even a cockroach, and certainly not this author, ever uncovers the whole picture or unearths the whole truth about the past. Why not? Well, a wonderful teacher once told me to think of the truth as a giant crystal ball that has fallen to Earth and shattered. Every time people find a tiny piece of the ball, they shout, "I've got the truth!" But they really only have a little crystal shard. In prehistoric history, these shards are particularly hard to find because everything happened so long ago, and dinosaurs didn't write anything down.

Elizabeth Levy

In this book, I piece together some precious bits of North America's prehistoric life: the fascinating, the horrible, the weird, the absolutely awesome, and the positively wacky. History is all of that, and I think we learn better when we can laugh a little. That same wonderful teacher of mine also told great jokes. He would have agreed that history can be wacky. So welcome to *America's Horrible Histories!*

Elizabeth Levy

Hi, Everybody!

Mel Roach here, and the pleasure is alllll mine. Who am I kidding? The pleasure is always mine, since nobody's ever really too happy to see a cockroach. I don't know why we got such a bad rap, but we sure did. Every time people turn on a light, I've got to run away before they take off a shoe and try to squash me.

But we roaches are tough. We've survived worse: killer meteors, angry volcanoes, terrible tidal waves, and even ferocious animals with teeth seven inches long! Imagine the shoe size you'd need to squash an animal with teeth that long! And I haven't even started talking about the dinosaurs yet. Yep, I've seen them all. Read on and you'll see this isn't just some roach rant. Of all the animals that have ever existed on Earth, I've been around about the longest — which makes me the perfect tour guide for your trip through history. Like that nice lady Liz, who wrote this book, says: Kick off your shoes (but watch where you put them!) and find a comfortable place to sit, because we're about to give you the real scoop about American history (and we're not just talking dinosaur dung here!). You won't believe what was going on before

you people came along. By the way, if you're going to eat anything while you're reading, don't be afraid to let a few crumbs fall on the floor. Your parents may not like it, but you'll make a cockroach or two very happy.

Remember, the name's Mel Roach, and I'm at your service. Now, let's find out what kind of animal has seven-inch teeth. Whatever it was, it must have spent a fortune on toothpaste!

Chapter 1
See the USA . . . On a Dinosaur

About 250 million years ago, the United States, all of the Americas — in fact, all of the world — was part of one humongous continent surrounded by a huge ocean. This supercontinent containing all the land on Earth is called Pangaea. The giant continent was hot, dry, and nasty. (Most of the United States was desert.) It was filled with cockroaches, scorpions, and reptiles. *Big* reptiles — like dinosaurs!

TIME LINE

250 million years ago
All the land on Earth is one big supercontinent called Pangaea

240 million years ago
Permian extinction

225 million years ago
Reptiles and dinosaurs first appear

220 million years ago
Triassic extinction

200 million years ago
Pangaea splits; North America drifts

14

"I Am the Greatest!"

Pangaea began to split apart about 200 million years ago or so. North America drifted along with all its inhabitants: dinosaurs, cockroaches, scorpions, and little mammals. Dinosaurs were the biggest of them all, but they also came in all different sizes: small, medium, large, and for a few extra bucks, "supersize." As a group, they got bigger and bigger while the little mammals rarely grew more than rat-sized. Dinosaurs were number one on the food chain and they stayed there for 150 million years, longer

Oooooo. . . buddy, that was so cold-blooded. In about 100,000,000 years, you're going to be sooooo sorry!

than any other species in history. Dinosaurs could snack on any mammal — but almost nothing could eat a dinosaur except another dinosaur.

North America's Early Dinosaurs: Small Is Beautiful

When dinosaurs started out on the supercontinent Pangaea, some of them were no bigger than chickens but probably not quite as tasty. Footprints of these small dinosaurs were preserved forever in desert sand that turned into rock. The northeast coast of North America, especially in what is now New England and New Jersey, is a particularly good place to find early dinosaur tracks from the age of Pangaea.

Don't Look Now, but Your Continent Is Drifting

You are here. . . . or at least you will be in about 100,000 years.

Throughout the Earth's history, land masses have split, collided, and split again. Forces inside the planet cause the continents to move at speeds of one to a few inches a year, about as fast as your fingernails grow. The continents move because the Earth's crust is divided into large plates that float on a soft layer of goo called the mantle. All of us living on continental plates move around as if we are drifting on inflatable rafts in a swimming pool.

You probably don't notice that the continent underneath you is moving, but even today, it's secretly playing a game of bumper car. A *very* slow game of bumper car. In fact, the continent is moving so slowly, it's actually a little more like waiting in line to get *on* the bumper cars. North America is moving farther away from Europe. In the year 2000, the Atlantic Ocean is 30 feet wider than it was when Columbus crossed over in 1492.

Whoa! Didn't America used to be here?

Ah, man! I'm wearing my good Italian shoes!

17

One of the oldest North American dinosaur fossils yet discovered is *Chindesaurus*. *Chinde* is a Native American word that means "ghost." *Chindesaurus* means "ghost lizard." Maybe it wasn't the biggest dinosaur around, but should we assume it was a "friendly" ghost lizard? *Chindesaurus* lived in Arizona nearly 200 million years ago when the United States was still part of Pangaea. Dinosaurs may have started out small, but everyone knows they didn't stay that way.

Says Who?

So who is making all these discoveries about fossils and dinosaur tracks? Well, anyone may

Dinosaur State Park in Rocky Hill, Connecticut, has hundreds of early dinosaur tracks. **Walter T. Kidde Memorial Dinosaur Footprint Quarry** in Roseland, New Jersey, is also a good place to see dinosaur footprints. **Petrified Forest National Park** is located in northeast Arizona about two hours east of Flagstaff. You can see petrified plants from the age of Pangaea.

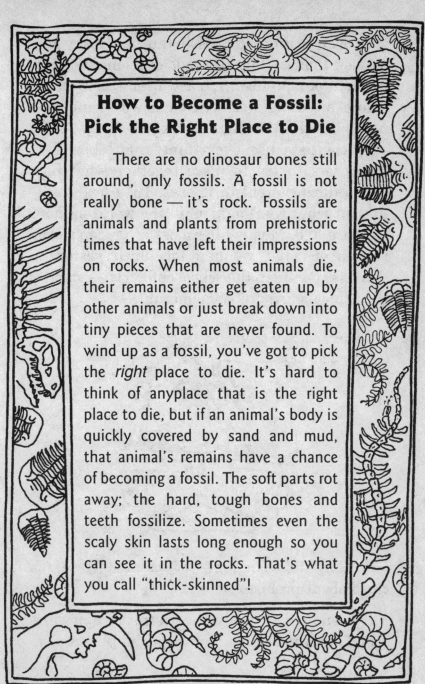

How to Become a Fossil: Pick the Right Place to Die

There are no dinosaur bones still around, only fossils. A fossil is not really bone — it's rock. Fossils are animals and plants from prehistoric times that have left their impressions on rocks. When most animals die, their remains either get eaten up by other animals or just break down into tiny pieces that are never found. To wind up as a fossil, you've got to pick the *right* place to die. It's hard to think of anyplace that is the right place to die, but if an animal's body is quickly covered by sand and mud, that animal's remains have a chance of becoming a fossil. The soft parts rot away; the hard, tough bones and teeth fossilize. Sometimes even the scaly skin lasts long enough so you can see it in the rocks. That's what you call "thick-skinned"!

trip over a dinosaur fossil (anyone lucky *and* clumsy, that is), but all kinds of scientists try to unearth our prehistoric past. Prehistoric means before anything was written down — and definitely before TV or the Internet.

Scientists use everything from shovels to computers to try to piece together what happened during prehistoric eras. They love to figure out what was going on in the world millions of years ago. Meanwhile, most of us can't even remember what we had for lunch yesterday. (Unless you ate in the school cafeteria — some of those meals are pretty memorable!)

Man, I just hate insect surprise day.

Many different kinds of scientists research clues about prehistoric times:

• *Paleontologists* study the fossils of dinosaurs and other prehistoric animals and plants.

- *Geologists* study the history, origin, and structure of the Earth.

- *Geophysicists* study the Earth's crust and how it moves.

- *Geomorphologists* study the landscapes on top of the Earth's crust and what changes them. (Geology is from the Greek word for the "study of earthly things," and "morph" means to change.)

- *Archaeologists* try to figure out how prehistoric people lived, based on what they left behind. So, never litter — we don't want future archaeologists to think we were a bunch of slobs!

The Big Plant-Eaters

Two huge extinctions killed off nearly 90 percent of the species on the supercontinent Pangaea and in the seas. The first one happened about 240 million years ago, and the other one around 20 million years later. The early dinosaurs survived both extinctions. And, yup, the cockroach did, too. So did many primitive plants, such as giant horsetails, ferns, and pine trees. The dinosaurs thought these plants were yummy, and they didn't have much competition in gathering them. Little competition meant lots of food to eat.

North America's biggest dinosaurs ate plants, not meat. Many of these huge, plant-eating dinosaurs were part of the sauropod family. Sauropods had very long necks, which made it easy to reach the most tender pine needles on tall tree-tops, but hard to shop for scarves.

Look up at the sixth floor of a building. That's where your head would be if you were one of America's biggest dinosaurs, say a *Sauroposeidon*. In the 1990s, scientists found neck fossils of this 60-foot dinosaur in Oklahoma. Its name is Latin for "earthquake god lizard."

Another of the largest dinosaur fossils yet discovered is the hipbone of an *Ultrasaurus* found in Colorado. The hipbone alone weighed 1,500 pounds, and paleontologists think that this Colorado dinosaur might have weighed over 100 tons. A ton equals 2,000 pounds, so that means that *Ultrasaurus* would have tipped the scales at over 200,000 pounds! (But since *Ultrasaurus* was always very sensitive about its weight, the other dinosaurs agreed not to kid around about those hips!)

> Hey!
> Get out of my salad!

Some sauropod fossils have stones in them, in the area where the dinosaur's stomach would have been. These rocks are called gastroliths or gizzard stones. Scientists believe these sauropods swallowed gizzard stones to grind the food in their stomachs, the same way some birds do today. Many scientists believe that birds are "living dinosaurs," modern descendants of the dinosaurs. Lucky for us, most birds are pretty

> Man! Unless you're a dinosaur or a bird, don't try eating rocks! Big mistake . . . no, really . . . BIG mistake! OOooooo!

23

What your dog thinks.

What your Stegosaurus thinks.

small and pretty easy to make friends with, as long as you have some bread crumbs and know how to whistle.

Many of the plant-eating dinosaurs were not exactly the brainiest animals on Earth. *Stegosaurus,* whose fossils are found only in North America, is famous for the spiny plates on its back. *Stegosaurus* is not famous for its brain. Though its body weighed over two tons (that's 4,000 pounds), *Stegosaurus*'s brain was the size of a walnut or a couple of tablespoons of peas and weighed about 2¼ ounces, making it the world's first "pea brain." The nearest that *Stegosaurus* came to a brainstorm was probably a light drizzle.

Forever Dung

Scientists try to find out about what dinosaurs ate by looking at their poop or dung. Some dinosaur poop has survived as fossils. Fossilized feces or dinosaur dung are called coprolites. One coprolite that's been found is nearly a foot long. (Ouch!!!!) After 100 million years, dinosaur dung doesn't smell like poop. It smells like rocks, for which scientists are extremely grateful.

The Flesh-eating Dinosaurs

Not all American dinosaurs ate plants. Some dinosaurs ate flesh, the meat from other dinosaurs or mammals. *Tyrannosaurus rex* was one of the biggest and heaviest of these meat-eating dinosaurs. *T. rex* stood about 20 feet high and may

What do you get when dinosaurs crash their cars?

Tyrannosaurus wrecks.

have weighed up to six tons, or 12,000 pounds. So far, North America is the only place where its fossils have been found. Lucky us!

T. rex is often portrayed as an aggressive animal on the attack, kind of like a man-eating tiger with scales. But take a look at its puny little arms. With arms that short, how much of a killer could *T. rex* have been? That dinosaur couldn't grab anything! In fact, if dinosaurs had to survive by boxing one another, *T. rex* would have had to change its name to KO.

T. rex had small arms and tiny eyes but a huge space in its skull for its smelling sense

No.

No.

No biting, huh?

Can I kick?

Are you sure I can't bite?

organs. A vulture also has a huge nasal space in its skull. Vultures can smell something dead up to 25 miles away. This hardly seems like a talent you'd *want* to have, but some scientists think that America's ferocious *T. rex* probably got most of its meals the same way vultures and hyenas do — by eating corpses. Other scientists point out that *T. rex*'s teeth are unusually strong and that this dinosaur could have killed with just one bite.

Most North American meat-eating dinosaurs were smaller than *T. rex* but probably much more dangerous. *Deinonychus* lived around 113 million years ago. This dangerous dinosaur weighed about 130 pounds and stood about five feet tall, with teeth shaped like daggers and a huge razor-sharp claw

Gee! You mammals just couldn't get a break back then!

on each foot. Yikes! Although *Deinonychus* hunted tiny ratlike mammals, it also hunted other dinosaurs. *Deinonychus* fossils are found mostly in Wyoming and Montana, along with the fossils of a lot of less fortunate dinosaurs that got in its way.

Paper or plastic?

A Dinosaur Named Sue

In 1997, the Field Museum of Natural History in Chicago paid $8.4 million for one of the most complete fossils of a *T. rex* ever found. McDonalds and Walt Disney World Resort both chipped in to help the museum buy the fossil. Most of the money went to Maurice Williams, a Sioux, who owned the land where Sue was found. The fossil is named after Susan Hendrickson, the scientist who found it. In summary, Susan named Sue who was bought from a Sioux.

These fossilized bones are helping scientists figure out how the North American *T. rex* lived. The Field Museum will display Sue's 250-bone skeleton. Two life-size models of this *T. rex* will tour McDonalds restaurants around the world; another replica of Sue will be placed at Dinoland USA in Disney World.

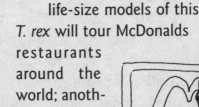

Now, you folks just relax and enjoy your lunch.

New Ideas About Very Old Creatures

Some of the most recent scientific discoveries have changed the way paleontologists think about dinosaurs. For example, in Montana's badlands, the tracks of several *Deinonychus* were found right next to the fossils of a much bigger plant-eating dinosaur, *Tenontosaurus*, which probably weighed around 20 tons. How could a 130-pound *Deinonychus* bring down a dinosaur that weighed 40,000 pounds? If you guessed "not by itself," you're right! Scientists think the tracks suggest that meat-eating dinosaurs hunted in packs, the same way wolves hunt today. In fact, think of them as the original pack animal. Most

How wolves got their moves.

Seeking Fossils Down by the Seashore

When the plate carrying the United States and the rest of North America began to drift away from Pangaea, it didn't just split off from the supercontinent. North America also nearly split in two. The movement of the plates pushed the young Rocky Mountains up out of the earth. An inland sea spread over much of what is now the United States. This inland sea cut off the new Rocky Mountains (which were actually just small bumps) in the west from the main part of the continent to the east. In some places, the inland sea was 2,000 miles wide. You would have needed an ocean liner to get from Salt Lake City to St. Louis. But as we all know from seeing the movie *Titanic*, boarding an ocean liner doesn't guarantee you'll get where you were going.

The edges of the inland sea were sandy and muddy — perfect for creating fossils. That's why Utah and Colorado and the badlands area of Montana and the Dakotas are still great places for finding dinosaur fossils. They are some of richest dinosaur fossil sites in the world.

Yes, I'm sure it's a totally cool seashell. Yes, you can bring it to school tomorrow. Now let Uncle Mel get some sleep, okay?

His food fights back and I'm the stupid one?

modern reptiles are solitary creatures, so the idea that dinosaurs might have hunted in packs surprised paleontologists.

Being killed by a pack of clawed dinosaurs would not have been pretty. (Although being killed by a pack of dinosaurs *without* claws wouldn't look much better.) The *Tenontosaurus* probably didn't die right away but went into shock while the pack of *Deinonychus* ripped at it with teeth and claws. Sounds yucky? It probably was! Still, *Deinonychus*, like almost all meat-eating creatures, killed only for food.

Meat-eating dinosaurs had better eyesight than plant eaters. Most meat eaters also had bigger brains because it's harder to hunt and kill a moving animal than it is to nibble plants that stay still.

North America Blossoms

About 100 million years ago, something happened that changed the world, not to mention the diet of plant-eating dinosaurs. For the first time, the world saw flowers.

Scientists believe that flowering plants are one of nature's most successful experiments: There are more than 200,000 different species of flowering plants around today. A lot of them might make you sneeze, but they sure are pretty to look at!

Flowers changed life in North America more than you might think. Besides looking good, flowers created many new foods. Picture your favorite dinosaur munching on a dogwood or a magnolia (the relatives of today's magnolias were among the first flowers). Dinosaurs seem to have had no trouble adjusting to snacking on flowers. Of course, considering they used to eat one another, pretty much anything seems like a step up.

A lot more insects joined the cockroaches and scorpions. Most of these insects had wings and could fly. They flitted from flower to flower. Some of them got stuck along the way. Many prehistoric insects are preserved in amber, a sticky sap that mainly comes from pine trees. As amber hardens, it preserves anything that gets stuck in it — in incredible detail. Because of its piney areas, New Jersey has some of the richest prehistoric amber deposits in the world, including a little mosquito with a mouth tough enough to bite through a dinosaur's skin and suck its blood. Scientists are just itching to get that mosquito to tell its prehistoric tale. It's nice to know these kinds of mosquitoes were once around, but it's even nicer to know their modern descendants aren't quite so tough!

Hey, kids! This is your great, great, great, great, great, great, great, great, great, great uncle, Torg. He still looks pretty good.

Looking for early insects in amber? Check out the **New Jersey State Museum,** in Trenton, New Jersey, and the **Rutgers Geology Museum** in New Brunswick, New Jersey. Both have collections of prehistoric insects caught in amber, in addition to many dinosaur fossils. The **Great Swamp Outdoor Education Center,** Great Swamp National Wildlife Refuge, Chatham Township, New Jersey, also has a display of dinosaur footprints from the time of flowering plants.

North America's Late Dinosaurs

By about 70 million years ago, the great inland sea in North America had almost dried up — for a while. Swamps and inland lakes dotted what are now the Midwest states. More and

I'm late! Now I'm going to go extinct for sure!

Hey there, buddy. Here in Nebraska, we all pretty much stopped using the diving board when the ocean dried up.

more flowering plants grew along these lands and swamps. North America's dinosaurs kept changing as the land around them changed.

The dinosaurs of this period came in all sorts of shapes. Many were about the size of an adult human. Others were four-legged tanklike creatures about the size of a cow. Still others went in for the horned look.

The Hadrosaurs:
Have Horn, Will Travel

Among the last dinosaurs to evolve in the Americas were the hadrosaurs, known for their weirdly shaped heads, often in the shape of a crest or horn that looks like a duckbill. Scientists think that the hadrosaurs might have used this headgear to make noises, blowing air through it like a saxophone. No human ever heard a

dinosaur, but dinosaurs had ear canals, so they could hear, and they probably made a lot of different noises. Elephants can communicate with one another by powerful, ultralow vibrations that they make in their skulls. Some scientists think the hadrosaurs used the bony crests on their head to "talk" to one another. Like most other animals, dinosaurs probably made noises when they were trying to attract a dinosaur of the opposite sex.

Hadrosaurs may have been among the last dinosaurs on Earth, but theirs were the first dinosaur fossils ever found in America. A hadrosaur fossil was uncovered in New Jersey in 1858. That's why *Hadrosaurus foulkii* is the official state dinosaur of New Jersey.

More New Ideas About
Very Old Creatures

The late dinosaurs fascinate scientists because there were so many different kinds of them. The more paleontologists learn about the late dinosaurs, the more they see that dinosaurs are very different from most modern reptiles.

The most obvious difference, of course, is that today's reptiles aren't six stories tall! For another thing, modern reptiles are not very social. Your average snake is not a party animal. Most modern reptiles lay eggs in solitary nests and walk, crawl, or slither away. For example, when most baby snakes hatch from their eggs, they're on their own.

In the 1970s, paleontologists discovered two large nesting sites in Montana. Each contained several nests of dinosaur eggs, right next to the

fossils of adults and young of various ages. Paleontologists were excited because they believed this evidence showed that dinosaurs took care of their young, the way birds take care of their babies. The fact that relatives of the ferocious *T. rex* were also loving parents may be the earliest proof that looks can be deceiving.

Dinosaur footprints found in places as far apart as Texas and Canada seem to show that dinosaurs might have lived in herds. The footprints of these herds show that dinosaurs may have protected their young by keeping them in the middle of the group, the way elephants do today. This, too, is very different from modern reptiles — which are pretty much loners.

As scientists look more closely at the way dinosaurs lived, they've begun to wonder whether dinosaurs really were cold-blooded, the way other reptiles are. Cold-blooded animals like reptiles need to warm up in the sun before they can move into action, which is why it's always nicer to run into a snake that's lying in the shade. There are a lot of advantages to being cold-blooded, particularly during a period when the Earth was warm, as it was during the dinosaurs' time. Cold-blooded animals need less food, and they generally live much longer than warm-blooded animals. Some dinosaurs might have lived longer than 100 years.

Sure he's cute now. But, man! The teething is nasty!

There are disadvantages to being warm-blooded like you, me, and all mammals. Mammals have to eat a lot to keep their temperature up.

Mmmm. . . that sounds pretty tasty. Could you hand me one of those really big toothpicks and a napkin?

What a rat race! These little mammals work so hard, like they think someday they'll be anything more than just hors d'oeuvres. That's so cute!

Warm-blooded animals need ten times more food than cold-blooded animals. Lucky for us there are way more than ten times the number of restaurants around now than there were when the dinosaurs lived.

Do you know one of these things eats as much as I do? Yet I can still eat a whole bunch of them! Wish I could figure this out, but my brain is the size of a nut.

Some scientists believe that dinosaurs might be an as-yet-unknown mixture of warm-blooded and cold-blooded. But whether they were warm-blooded or cold-blooded, nothing could save the dinosaurs from what was coming next. It was going to change the prehistoric world forever!

America is so rich in dinosaur fossils that almost all museums of natural history have dinosaur exhibits. Here are a few places to see scientists at work still discovering dinosaurs.

Dinosaur National Monument in Dinosaur, Colorado

Cleveland-Lloyd Dinosaur Quarry in Price, Utah

Dinosaur Provincial Park in Patricia, Alberta, Canada

The **American Museum of Natural History** in New York City (often sponsors hands-on classroom dinosaur adventures for kids)

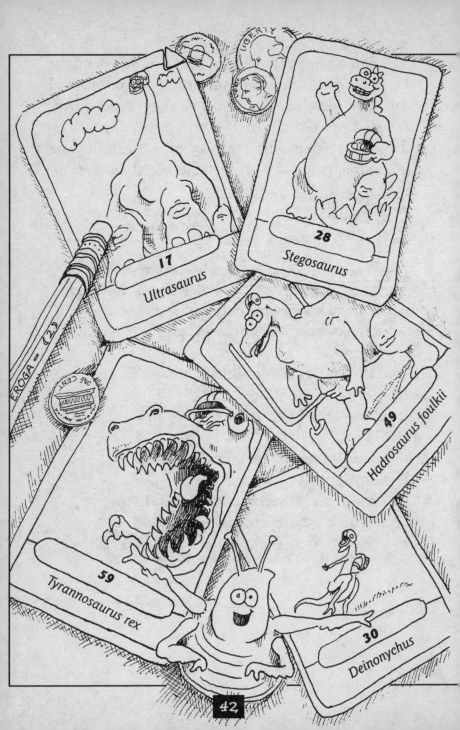

Wearing# 49, coming

straight from the swamps, New Jersey's own bad boy, *Hadrosaurus foulkii!*

#17 is from the great state of Colorado and is 100 tons of vegetarian terror . . . it's *Ultrasaurus!*

At 4,000 pounds, with a brain the size of a walnut, what #28 lacks in intelligence, he makes up for in courage. The plant eater with a purpose . . . *Stegosaurus!*

#59 is the most famous member of our squad. A 20-foot meat eater with short arms and an even shorter temper. Everybody better cheer for *Tyrannosaurus rex!*

#30 has razor-sharp teeth and claws but stands just five feet tall and weighs only 130 pounds. We call him "Rudy" but his real name is *Deinonychus!*

There you have it: some of the American Dinos. Now let's give them a big hand because here's a hot tip — they aren't going to be around for very long.

Chapter 2
Dinosaurs Die, Meteor Blamed

Many scientists believe that one day about 65 million years ago, a huge rock from outer space, about four to nine miles wide, raced toward Earth. Something dramatic started happening at that time (and we're not talking about a Shakespeare festival!). Fossil records show that *all* the dinosaurs, not just the ones in North America, but every species around the world died out then. And not only the dinosaurs dropped dead. *All* land animals that weighed over 55 pounds went kaput. So did some smaller animals,

TIME LINE

65 million years ago
All the dinosaurs die; many other species die, too

65 million years ago (one minute earlier)
A little-known dinosaur called the *Psychicsaurus* gets a

weird feeling something terrible is going to happen

I ain't like udder meteors! I never kilt nobody. It's a frame-up, I tells ya! I was framed!

too. All the pterosaurs and other flying reptiles croaked. In the sea, it was even worse. Creature after creature went belly-up. Most became extinct and were never seen on Earth again. Seventy-five percent of all the Earth's species, both plants and animals, disappeared 65 million years ago. Since there's no evidence that magic was widely practiced by the dinosaurs, we can safely assume this wasn't a trick.

In 1998, the **American Museum of Natural History** in New York City opened a brand-new permanent exhibit on biodiversity and how species survive or go extinct. If you like animals and science, you shouldn't miss it.

Smarts, Farts, or Pardon My Meteor

The death of the dinosaurs, after 150 million years of world domination, is one of history's great mysteries. This extinction divides two great periods of time: the Cretaceous Period, the last period for the great lizards, and the Tertiary Period, the first age of mammals. Scientists call this

---

Extinct Stinks

Species have come and gone throughout the Earth's history, but there are five times in the history of the Earth when almost all life went extinct. These are known as the Five Big Extinctions.

Extinct Stinks #1 — Ordovician: About 439 million years ago, before there was much life on land, early life in the sea almost all died off. Scientists think it was because the Earth and the sea became cooler.

Extinct Stinks #2 — Devonian: By about 364 million years ago, the first forests had grown up on land and the first animals had crawled out of the sea. Amphibious animals like the salamander, which can live both in land and water, were almost wiped out. No one knows exactly why.

Extinct Stinks #3 — Permian: 240 million years ago, nearly 90 percent of the species on Earth were wiped out.

Extinct Stinks #4 — Triassic: 220 million years ago, even more early mammals and other animals on Pangaea

extinction the K-T extinction. K stands for Kreide, a chalk that was found in rocks at the end of the Cretaceous Period. (Another great mystery is why scientists didn't make it simple and call it the C-T extinction.)

How could the largest and most successful land animals of all time just suddenly disappear?

died out. Reptiles like the dinosaurs took over.

Extinct Stinks #5: Cretaceous or K-T Extinction:
About 65 million years ago, the dinosaurs died out along with many other species. Most scientists now think the Earth was hit by a giant asteroid or comet.

Many scientists believe that the Earth is now going through a sixth extinction because one species, humans, are hogging so much of the world's resources. So we could be facing:

Extinct Stinks #6 — The 21st Century!
(But let's hope not!)

Watch me pull a pterosaur out of my hat. HEY!! What the . . .

Here are a few of the theories scientists have put forth about what happened to all those dinosaurs.

Mammals Were More Fit Than Dinosaurs

One theory said that mammals were smarter than dinosaurs. According to this idea, mammals were more fit to survive; they evolved and dinosaurs didn't.

Survival of the Fittest

In other words, prehistoric mammals just got smarter and smarter, and they took over from the dinosaurs. (Humans are mammals. It's nice to think that we survived because we were smarter.)

There's just one problem with this theory. Scientists now know that dinosaurs changed even more than mammals did during the 150 million years that these giant reptiles ruled the Earth. They didn't exactly build schools and railroads, but they *did* change. So why would dinosaurs suddenly stop evolving?

Dinosaurs Got Too Big for Their Own Good

Some scientists believed the dinosaurs became extinct because they just got too big. According to this theory, dinosaurs began to get slipped disks

and bad backs and then had trouble mating. The problem with this theory is that many of the late dinosaurs were smaller than the huge sauropods. Why would these smaller dinosaurs all suddenly die out? (P.S. These are hard questions with no easy answers, so don't feel bad if you don't know the solutions, not even the greatest scientists in the world do, either.)

Too Many Dinosaurs Breaking Wind at Once

According to this theory, there were so many dinosaurs that they killed themselves off with their own flatulence or breaking wind. (Farting is the word most of us use, even if it is a little impolite.) Flatulence comes from gas in the intestines. When an animal lets the gas go into the air, methane escapes. This has probably happened to you, although I doubt your gas ever killed anybody — at least I *hope* not!

Methane is a gas that can cause the Earth's atmosphere to warm up. So many dinosaurs, so much methane! However, the animals in the oceans didn't stand downwind from a dinosaur breaking wind, yet many fish and other creatures in the ocean also died out 65 million years ago. Most scientists think the flatulence theory is full of hot air.

The Earth Got Too Cool

A lot of volcanoes started erupting and blowing lava into the air around 65 million years ago. The ash from the volcanoes might have caused temperatures to drop by darkening the skies, making it hard for dinosaurs to live, let alone get a decent suntan!

The Earth Got Too Hot

The Earth had been gradually warming up toward the end of the dinosaur era. Just a few degrees change could have made life tough for the dinosaurs. Even if the dinosaurs were cold-blooded, they

might not have been able to survive the warmer weather. The problem with this theory is that dinosaurs had already survived many slightly different temperatures during their 150 million years on Earth. So again, why would all of them die out? If you can figure this out, please call your nearest scientists, because they're dying to know.

Something From Outer Space Hit the Earth

Even before the 1980s, many scientists suspected that the dinosaurs died out because the Earth was hit by something from outer space. The problem was that there was no proof . . . yet!

Hello, dinosaurs! It's me, Mel. You know how I was supposed to blow up that meteor? Well, the funniest thing happened . . . uh, I'll tell you about it when I get there—which will be in about a minute!

Proof Behind the Meteor Theory

In the last few decades, more and more evidence has been uncovered supporting the idea that dinosaurs died a fiery death when a meteor struck Earth. In the 1970s, a father-and-son team, geologists Luis and Walter Alvarez, discovered that rocks all over the world had a layer rich in iridium in them. Iridium is not an expensive pest-control service. It's an element not often found on Earth but very common in meteors. This iridium layer was laid down on Earth around 65 million years ago, about the same time that the dinosaurs died. Only a giant meteor could have spilled that much iridium.

You kids! Again with the iridium tracked all over my kitchen!

The Alvarez theory started a hunt for a crater big enough to be proof of such a massive, destructive meteor hit. Eventually, scientists discovered a giant crater called Chicxulub. It is buried under the sea, off the North American coast between Texas and Mexico. Chicxulub is nearly 200 miles across. No other crater on Earth or even on Venus or Mars is that large. Scientists had missed it because most of Chicxulub is underwater and everyone knows scientists are afraid of the water. (That's not true, but it would be funny if it was.)

In the 1990s, scientists tested rock samples from Chicxulub. They found the crater was indeed blasted out 65 million years ago. Scientists then tried to re-create what might have happened when the meteor hit. They made computer models of atomic blasts and volcanoes. Using a mathematical formula, the computers designed a blast that would gouge a hole the size of Chicxulub. Scientists found out Chicxulub was so big that it would take a normal volcano 500,000 years to generate the energy that jolted the Earth in just one minute of meteor impact!

When the meteor hit the Earth's atmosphere, parts of it would have broken off. In 1998, scientists found what they believe is an actual piece of the original meteor. It was found on the floor of the Pacific Ocean off the California coast. How about that? After all the time spent looking for a piece of meteor, all those scientists had to do was look on the floor!

The colossal meteor would have been so bright that it must have looked like a second sun as it raced toward the Earth. Since Superman wasn't even born yet, there was no one around who was brave enough to destroy the space menace before it hit the Earth, and so . . . BOOM! The colossal rock tore through the atmosphere and plunged into the ocean off the coast of Mexico. In North America, the dinosaurs must have felt the earth shake underneath them. Burning pieces of the meteor fell down on forests and the trees burst into flames. The sky turned black with smoke. A wall of water thousands of feet high thundered into the Gulf Coast. This tidal wave doused some of the forest fires, but it also drowned everything in its path — everything! Well, maybe not every single cockroach and every single ratlike mammal, but almost every other living creature in Mexico, Texas, Louisiana, Arkansas, and Florida would have died — especially the ones that couldn't surf!

Some dinosaurs probably survived the fires, but forest fires are incredibly dirty. Most North American dinosaurs were probably covered with ash within days of the meteor landing. Within a week, the world's air must have been thick with dust and smoke. Ash blocked out the sun. There was so much dust in the air that very little light could get through. The rain that fell with the dust was full of acid from the fires. More and more plants would have died, leaving the surviving dinosaurs less and less food to eat.

The temperatures got colder and colder because the warm rays from the sun couldn't pierce through the dust. Many dinosaurs, probably most of them cold-blooded, would have frozen to death. Some dinosaurs may have survived a year or two or even much, much longer, but not long enough to save the species. Scientists have now figured out that you don't have to kill off *all* of a species for an animal or plant to become extinct. There's what they call a "kill curve." This means that even if

Dear Reader
I was supposed to appear on this page, but I figured with all the fire, the acid rain, the meteors, and tidal waves... FORGET ABOUT IT! I'll catch you on another page
Love Mel

P.S. this sort of fore-thought is why I have friends living under your sink and dinosaurs don't!

Single, greenish-blue widowed female seeking single, greenish-blue male. Must be easygoing, professional, and have good sense of humor; 30 feet tall a plus. And . . . who am I kidding? If you're alive, call me!

a few animals survive, there aren't enough of them to really reproduce, and the species eventually disappears.

If ever a nuclear war broke out, the Earth would probably look very much the way it did to the dying dinosaurs. Scientists call this desolation a "nuclear winter," because they believe it is what the world would be like after a nuclear war.

No one knows exactly how long it took all the dinosaurs to die. Maybe it was just 100 years, maybe it was thousands of years. Some scientists argue that it took even longer. Others say that the killer meteor scene is not the way it happened at all, that it might have been a comet that caused all the destruction. But all scientists agree on one thing — although dinosaurs may

have survived as birds, the giant class of animals that had so dominated the landscape for 150 million years was gone forever.

Dinosaurs lay dying everywhere. Bugs, including of course the cockroach, survived the meteor blast. In fact, very few insects showed signs of extinction. It's amazing. You can stomp a bug out with your foot, but somehow they can survive meteor crashes and tidal waves.

Insects ate the decaying vegetation. Many little rat-like mammals also survived. They were already used to eating bugs and now there were more insects than ever to swallow. (Isn't it weird how swallowing insects suddenly sounds like a good thing?) These little mammals also had furry bodies so they could survive the cooler weather caused by the clouds of ashes blocking the sun. For nearly 150 million years, the little rodentlike mammals had lived in the shadows of the mighty dinosaurs. Now it was the mammals' turn!

Boy, oh, boy, if this is Earth, it looks horrible! Somebody should really get a mop or call a janitor or something because I'm sure not going to clean up this mess. I mean, look at this place. There are insects everywhere, rats running around, and the sun never comes out.

At least there are no more dinosaurs. They were kind of cool to look at for the first 150 million years or so, but they were really starting to get on my nerves, stomping around here like their flatulence didn't stink. Heck, if that meteor or comet hadn't come around, their own smell would have killed them off for sure.

Oh, well. At least I'm alive and that's all that matters. Things may look pretty bleak right now, but something tells me the sun is going to come back

out, and the trees are going to grow taller than ever, and a whole new species of animals will be born, and the next 65 million years are going to be the best years of my life! Of course, I could be wrong. . . .

Chapter 3

Mammals' Time to Shine

After the meteor blast, the air eventually cleared and the sun shone. The dinosaurs were gone. The little mammals came out to play in the nice warm sun. Plants grew back. It was as if a huge feast was laid out.

Toward the end of the dinosaur age, the drifting continents shifted, making the weather warmer all over North America. Soon it was so warm and tropical in North America that crocodiles lolled in the Arctic circle in Alaska and palm trees grew in Wisconsin.

TIME LINE

65 million years ago
The sun comes back out; North America becomes a warm, lush rain forest

60 million years ago
Earth's colliding plates send the Rocky Mountains shooting up in western North America

40 million years ago
North America cools down; grass takes over. Some animals eat grass; others eat the grass eaters

Honey, the alligators are back. Could you go quick count the elves again?

The landscape of North America changed. The Earth's plates pushed the young Rockies up from hilly bumps to mountains. They soared even higher than they are today. A series of huge volcanoes erupted in these new mountains. They spit out ash that eventually turned into very rich soil full of plants for animals to munch on. North America was about to get some of the fattest mammals the world has ever seen.

Ever? Fattest mammal ever? Liz, come on. Didn't you see that guy on Jerry Springer?

20 million years ago
A lot of animals hoof it over what some people call the Beringia Bridge between Alaska and Siberia

20 million years ago (one hour later)
A lot of animals are late for work due to traffic on the Bridge

Here a Mammal, There a Mammal, Everywhere a Mammal, Mammal

A lot of the animals that we've come to love — horses, dogs, pigs, cats, elephants, monkeys, humans — all got their start after the dinosaurs died. Mammals no longer had to stay small to hide from dinosaurs. There was a lot more food and a lot less danger, so mammals developed in all sizes and shapes. Some were as big as a tank; others were as tiny as your thumb. Some were a little strange-looking, too. One North American mammal, *Eobasilius,* looked a little like a tank or a rhinoceros except it had six horns instead of one. Two horns were between its eyes, two were on its nose, and two were high on its forehead.

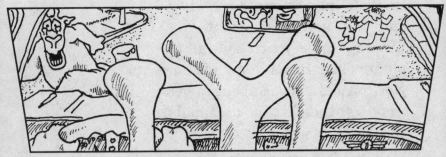

The viewpoint of the Eobasilius
(and why they drove cars very badly).

Horns help mammals attract a mate during daylight. Antlers are usually a way for a male to signal a female that he's around. It's the basic "hey, look at me" approach to the mating game.

Many mammals grew horns on their heads after the dinosaurs died because now they could mate and feast during the daytime — and not get eaten! (Pronghorn antelopes still go in for the big-branched look.) Horns or antlers also sometimes help defend a mammal against a meat-eating enemy.

The first horses the world ever saw developed in North America about 55 million years ago. They were about the size of fox terriers. These little horses lived in the swampy forest. They had four toes on their back legs and three toes on their front legs. They ran on tiptoes. Picture a lush rain forest: palm trees, soft rainfall, luscious fruit in trees, heavy ripe fruit falling to the ground. Picture yourself as a young ancestor of the modern horse. You live under the rain forest canopy. There's no grass to eat, but all that lush fruit is yours for the taking . . . provided it doesn't fall on your little head and knock you out. Your tiptoes help you run quickly across the rain forest floor, eating dangling leaves and fruit (even though your friends make fun of you for running that way). With no dinosaurs there to hog all the best food, you can really chow down.

The New Food Chain

Why did horses have to run fast? Why did mammals with horns need to defend themselves?

Because there were also a lot of brand-new meat-eating mammals around. Some of them are still with us.

The disappearance of the dinosaurs left a big hole at the top of the food chain, especially for meat-eating animals. *T. rex* was gone, and so were the other meat-eating dinosaurs that had hunted in packs. Still, it seems part of nature's plan that wherever plant-eating animals go, meat-eating animals follow. It was true in the dinosaur age, and it's still true today.

However, eating meat is very risky for most animals. It's easy to get hurt if you're trying to eat something that will slash you with its hoofs or spear you with its tusks. Meat-eating animals have to be able to catch and kill their prey without getting killed themselves. And just think, we get upset if there's a long line at the supermarket.

At the beginning of the mammal age, giant flightless birds of prey were among the scariest meat-eating mammals around. One of them, *Diatryma*, stood nearly seven feet

Why aren't they just called meatavores?

Nature's Plan
① Herbivores go where they want
② Make sure carnivores follow
③ Repeat

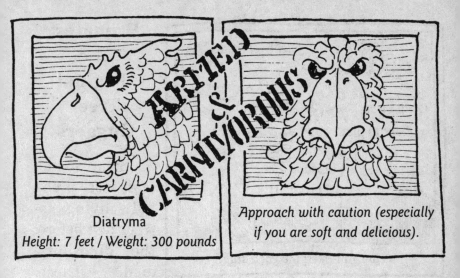

Diatryma
Height: 7 feet / Weight: 300 pounds

Approach with caution (especially if you are soft and delicious).

tall. It had a huge parrotlike beak and enormous claws. *Diatryma* could tear a little mammal like the early horse to pieces. In the bushy undergrowth of North America's rain forests, it was the number-one killer.

Other meat-eating predators were early versions of bears. *Andrewsarchus* was nearly twice as big as a grizzly bear. It had hooves like cattle, jaws like a crocodile, and was among the biggest meat-eating mammals of all time. *Andrewsarchus* lived along riverbanks and fished. After all, even meat eaters like a nice piece of fish now and then. Some scientists believe bearlike mammals such as *Andrewsarchus* developed into whales around 50 million years ago.

Living in trees: the good stuff.

Plenty of food

Great view

Place to play

Escape from predators

Living in trees: the bad stuff.

Gravity

Primates: The Original Tree-Huggers

Some mammals were probably living in trees just before the dinosaurs died. These mammals were the early primates. Primates are mammals that have a thumb or a big toe that moves separately from the other fingers and toes. The thumb and big toe make it easier to hold on to a branch in a tree. But more important, eventually they make it easier to stand up straight and eat a pizza. Primates also have fingernails and toenails and four incisor teeth. Some early primates had brains somewhat larger than other mammals. They also had blood systems that delivered more oxygen to their brains.

In North America there were nearly a dozen different species of early primates. They were mainly about the size of a house cat, many a lot smaller. Most ate insects and fruit they found on the trees in the rain forests. These little shrewlike primates had claws that helped them hold on to the branches. They also could move their arms in complete circles. Try spinning your arm in a circle, but absolutely do not ask your dog or cat to do this. No other mammal — except a primate like a monkey or an ape or a human — can do this without screaming in pain.

What's up with Frank?

He thinks he's better than us. Something about more oxygen going to his brain. I think he's just got a big head.

Denver Museum of Natural History in Denver, Colorado, has a great fossil record of many of America's early mammals. Also visit the Lila Acheson Wallace Wing of Mammals and Their Extinct Relatives at the **American Museum of Natural History** in New York City, right next to the dinosaurs on the fourth floor.

We can also do it while screaming in pain, but there's no point in that.

The ability to move an arm in a complete circle helped the primates swing through branches of trees. Eventually it would help one primate learn to throw a stone or a spear and later, a baseball, but that wouldn't happen just yet.

North America Gets a New Weather Report: Cool, with Snowflakes

Between 50 and 40 million years ago, North America's weather went from warm and sunny to cool and changeable. Guess what happened? The Earth's plates were moving around again. This time, the plate under Antarctica broke free from

South America and drifted toward the South Pole. Far from the equator and the sun's warmest rays, Antarctica froze over. Ice from the newly frozen Antarctica floated into ocean currents. It was one of the factors that cooled all of North America and the rest of the world. As more and more ice developed, it used up huge amounts of water. This created much more dry land along both coasts of North America.

Snowflakes began to fall over much of North America in the winter, but the snow melted in the spring. Because of the cool weather, a new plant came on the scene: grass. And those green blades really changed life in North America.

Grass: You Just Can't Keep a Good Plant Down

Grass grows very well when it's cool out, and it doesn't die when it's covered with snow. Wherever grass seeds drop on dirt, they sprout very quickly. That's why grass pops up in the cracks of sidewalks. What is really unusual about grass is the way it grows. Most plants sprout new leaves near their tops, the way trees do. But new grass leaves begin to grow near the bottom of the plant. For an animal, grass is like having a bottomless box of cereal to munch on. This is also why grass makes great lawns. If you tried to mow ivy, you'd end up with a bunch of dead stems.

> Grass. Yes, GRASS! See the big picture, my friend. A dynamic, challenging business opportunity, capable of manifesting itself into financial security beyond your wildest dreams!

The Grass Goes In, the Grass Goes Out . . . the Grass Goes . . .

Ever watch your dog or cat eat grass and then throw up? If you answered yes, maybe you should spend less time watching your pets. Cats and dogs are mostly meat eaters. Like humans, they can eat many different foods, but they can't break down grass in their stomachs. Grass is very hard to digest.

In order to let some animals eat grass, nature's solution is weird, but it works. Extra sacs in the stomach! Some grass-eating mammals, such as cattle, have as many as four chambers in their stomachs. Bison and cattle move the grass from one stomach sac to another. Meanwhile, they keep vomiting up the grass for more chewing. The polite term for this is "regurgitation" or "chewing the cud." The impolite term is "that completely disgusting thing that bison and cattle

Good things about grass

Bad things about grass

Looks like our little tough-guy carnivore can't hold his grass! I hope none of our friends sees this.

do with their food." It may sound disgusting to you, but the truth is . . . well, actually, it *is* pretty disgusting. But just because cattle and bison don't eat like you and me doesn't mean the way they chow down is wrong.

Extra chambers in your stomach are good places to keep food until it is safe to eat. A grazing mammal can stuff itself full of grass, then flee to a safer place to finish digesting. It's sort of like having a built-in refrigerator. Why were these grass eaters so worried about safety? Because other mammals got very good at pouncing on grazing animals. Relatives of those predators may be in your house right now.

What do you call a cow eating grass?

A lawn mooer.

Cats: Cute, Lethal, Built for Biting

Cats, even cute little kittens, are built for biting. They are descended from the many meat-eating mammals that developed at the same time as the grass eaters. *Nivaravus*, a leopardlike cat, hunted in the forests of North America 30 million years ago. Later, prehistoric saber-toothed cats were probably the most successful catlike hunters in North America. Most animals attack something about their equal in size, but not saber-toothed cats. A single saber-toothed cat could bring down an animal three times its size, even a mammoth bigger than an elephant. The saber-toothed cat, or *Smilodon*, was mistakenly called a tiger for years.

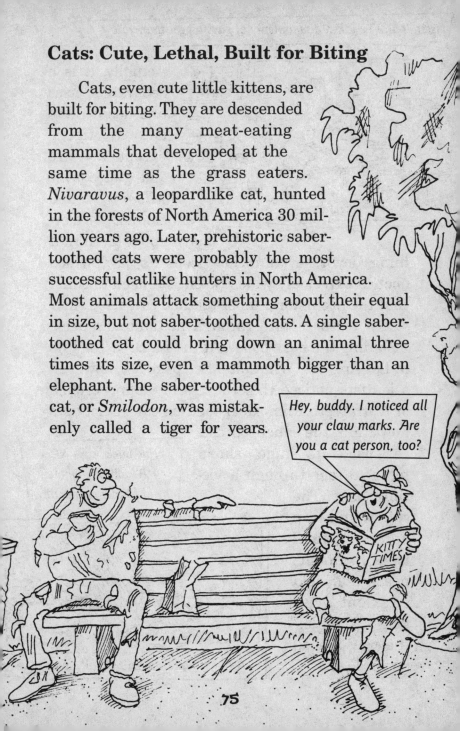

Hey, buddy. I noticed all your claw marks. Are you a cat person, too?

KITTY TIMES

Listen, pal. I've taken down plenty of guys bigger than you.

Actually, it is a separate species and has little to do with tigers, except its size and giant jaws. *Smilodon* had enormous, razor-sharp upper teeth that hung down seven inches from its jaw, which opened extremely wide. Scientists used to think that the prehistoric saber-toothed cats used their sharp teeth to bite through an animal's neck, including the neck bones. At the La Brea Tar Pits in Los Angeles (What pits? See page 99), however, scientists noticed that they rarely found broken or worn teeth from saber-toothed cats. Scientists now think the saber-toothed cat used its huge, sharp teeth to tear through a victim's belly. The cats would leap at an animal from underneath and hold on tight, getting "inside," the way a good boxer does.

Five bucks says NO WAY will my whole head fit in your mouth.

A metamynodon *really, really* loses a bet.

Dogs: Cute, Lethal, Built for Hunting in Packs

The ancestors of all dogs were mammals that hunted down grass eaters in packs, just as *Deinonychus* and other meat-eating dinosaurs hunted in packs. *Hesperocyon* was a meat-eating ancestor of jackals, wolves, and dogs that hunted about 30 million years ago. Wolves, including the dire wolf, came later as the weather turned cooler. Dire wolves were not much bigger than today's wolves. Like all

Hesperocyon *passed speed, strength, intelligence, and superkeen senses of hearing and smell on to modern dogs.*

Yo quiero some fur!

Some modern dogs seem to have been absent on the day they were being passed out.

wolves and even your dog, dire wolves had very sharp teeth that could cut through flesh and other teeth that could crush bones. Occasionally, dire wolves could even bring down an animal many times their size. The only animals that were safe from these fierce wolves were mammoths and mastodons. Just like today's elephants, mammoths and mastodons were so big that almost nothing, except a saber-toothed cat, could attack a full-grown adult.

The Mastodons and Mammoths Take in America

The elephantlike mastodons and mammoths did not develop in North America. They started out in Africa and branched out to Europe and

Asia. Mastodons were hairy, huge, and had trunks for grabbing leaves off trees. Just think of an elephant with a fur coat. They had teeth shaped like cones for munching down twigs, branches, and hard, woody forest vegetation. Mastodon comes from the Greek word for "nipple teeth" because that's what their teeth looked like — rows of nipples.

Mastodons first came to North America between 18 and 20 million years ago, via the

> *What's green, 6 feet 8 inches long, and weighs 37 pounds?*

Beringia Bridge. The Beringia Bridge isn't really a bridge. (If it was, its theme song might be "Bridge *Under* Troubled Waters"!) It's a land mass between Alaska and Siberia that is the floor of the Bering Sea.

A mastodon booger.

However, for millions of years, Beringia was *above* sea level; it was a grassy, wooded home to

Mastodon State Park in Imperial, Missouri. More than 60 mastodon skeletons have been recovered in Missouri. Mastodons also must have liked the environment in what is now New York State. Scientists think that hundreds of thousands of mastodons used to feast on the forests of New York State. More than 100 mastodon skeletons have been discovered throughout the state. Again, you can see mammoths and mastodons in the Lila Acheson Wallace Wing of the **American Museum of Natural History** in New York City.

huge herds of animals. In some places, Beringia was nearly 1,000 miles wide, about the same distance between Denver and Los Angeles.

Sitting between North America and Asia, Beringia became an animal superhighway. Mountain goats, bighorn sheep, oxen, bison, and deer, all prehistoric grass-eaters that are still around today, wandered to North America via Beringia. Horses and camels once native to North America sauntered across Beringia to Asia and from there into Europe. Horses didn't come back to North America until Columbus brought them on his second voyage. Camels returned much, much later, as attractions in circuses and zoos.

As soon as mastodons got to North America, they multiplied like bunnies. Mastodon remains can be found from Florida to New York, from Georgia to California. Mastodons were not the only animal with a trunk to find a happy home in America. They were followed by another elephantlike animal, the mammoth. The mammoth arrived in the middle of the ice age. Did they mind the cold? Naw. They didn't even mind the ice, which was a good thing because mammoths, mastodons, and all the other North American mammals were about to get their first ice age in a very long time.

I told you everything would turn out okay. Just look at this place now. It's amazing what a few million years and some light dusting can do, isn't it? It's so nice, even with all these interesting new animals that came over the Beringia Bridge to live here, including that one I told you about earlier with the seven-inch teeth! (That saber-tooth's not so bad when you get to know it.) Some of the new animals even have thumbs that must have come in handy if they had to hitchhike during their trip. There are monkeys, horses, pigs, and even dogs! (I was thinking about getting a puppy, but I'm probably best off waiting a little while, since they still have a tendency to hunt in packs and kill whatever they see.) There are even brand-new kinds of plants to eat and plenty of stomachs to put them in! But I'm not surprised. Like I've always said, "The grass is always greener on the other side of the Cretaceous Extinction." Although it is getting a little cold around here. . . .

Chapter 4
The Ice Age Cometh

At least one million years ago, North America got another new weather report: frigid with occasional warm periods. Ice ages don't happen slowly. They hit the Earth in jolts and jerks. Long before dinosaurs walked on this planet, the Earth had gone through dramatic ice ages. But for well over 200 million years, the Earth had stayed relatively warm. This was good news for all the animals, plus it made the weather person's job *really* easy.

3.5 million years ago
North America and South America smash into each other; North America gets much colder; ice no longer completely melts in the summer

1.7 to 1.5 million years ago
The mammoth family arrives

1 million years ago
The Beringia Bridge is submerged during warm periods

You say, "Let's stop for coffee."
I say, "The bridge doesn't look good."
You say, "Plenty of time."
I say, "Like there's no coffee in America?
Well, I sure hope that's some good
coffee you got there!"

What Causes an Ice Age?

Like so much of prehistoric history, the theories keep changing. Today, many scientists think that the movement of the Earth's plates triggered the most recent ice age.

About 3.5 million years ago, the plate carrying North America and the plate carrying South America collided and joined. When that happened, ocean winds got cut off by the land that we now call Panama. The winds blew cooler air

1 million to 12,000 years ago
North America is covered with ice sheets that come and go as far south as New York; animals do just fine until humans arrive

Yesterday
A little boy in Canada slips on the ice and falls on his butt; everyone laughs

onto the land. It's amazing how even little shifts in the planet change the weather.

About a million years ago, the moving plates between Alaska and Siberia collided and Beringia began to sink into the sea. Alaska and Siberia became separated by 55 miles of choppy water, the Bering Strait. This also shifted wind patterns and may have made the continent colder. More snow fell in Canada and the northern United States than could melt in the summer. Then the ice built up and made the weather even colder. Once ice gets started, it keeps piling up. Then it begins to move, sometimes in jerks and stops. The ice in the northern parts of the continent became thicker and heavier. Ice from the north began to creep south.

If ice keeps piling up, why is there always only one cube in my ice trays?

How Do Glaciers Crawl? Does Sliding on Your Bottom Sound Like Fun?

When glaciers get really thick, about as thick as a big, three-story house is high, gravity begins to pull the glaciers downhill. Meanwhile, the Earth is heated by radioactive energy coming from its core. This makes the glacier warmer at the bottom than it is at the top. As the glacial ice gets thicker and thicker, a pool of water forms on this warmer bottom of the glacier. These huge

Glacier! Oh, no! It's a glacier!!!!
Slither, everybody!
Slither for your lives!

mountains of ice sit on a surface that must feel a little like Vaseline. Glaciers literally slide on their bottoms. A typical glacier flows down a valley about 650 feet a year, or the length of some elementary schools. "Galloping glaciers" move in spurts and can travel four miles in just a few months. Still, even a galloping glacier is not really galloping. Most animals could get out of the way with just a brisk trot.

Because the weather stayed cool, glaciers slip slided into one another and formed even bigger glaciers. These gigantic glaciers kept the air cool, so more glaciers formed. Glacial ice also picked up huge boulders and carried them along. Ancient forests were mowed down as if by a giant electric lawn mower.

Most of North America was occasionally crushed by ice powerful enough to grind down huge mountains. During the coldest periods, ice covered almost all of Canada and most of the United States as far south as St. Louis. In New York City, the ice was so thick that it was taller than the Empire State Building. Near Chicago, the glaciers were sometimes more than two miles thick, taller than ten Empire State Buildings. Yet during most of the ice

age, Los Angeles never froze over. You could still have snorkeled in Florida. There was no ice there or in much of the South and Southwest United States.

Ice: The Great Interior Decorator

Glaciers changed much of the landscape of North America. Ice gouged out Puget Sound in Washington State. Ice created valleys in the middle of the Rocky Mountains. Skiers and snowboarders in Aspen, Colorado, slide down slopes carved out by a glacier. Rivers got dammed up by ice packs. The dammed-up rivers turned into enormous lakes; in fact, we call them the Great Lakes. (The Great Lakes are Huron, Ontario, Michigan, Erie, and Superior. Their first letters spell "Homes." Lake Champlain between New York and Vermont is a long lake also made by a glacier. Don't get me wrong. Champlain is a *decent* lake, it's just not a *great* lake.)

Hot and Sunny:
Not Everyone's Idea of an Ice Age

The ice age was *not* three million years of shivering animals and frozen glaciers. At least every 100,000 years or so, the climate would get warm again. Of course, keep in mind that 100,000 years is a long time, so it wasn't like the animals could just wait it out. Time and again, the glaciers would melt and the climate would warm up. The glaciers were kind of like a guest that stays for a long time, finally leaves, and then comes back again. Scientists now think that glaciers came and went even more often than had once been thought.

In between the glacier periods, it was at least as warm in most of North America as it is today. During these warm periods, the glaciers melted. Camels, rhinoceroses, horses, mammoths, and all the lions, dogs, bears, wolves, and saber-toothed cats that preyed on them would move onto the grasslands vacated by the glaciers. There were rhinoceroses in Nebraska and camels in Texas during the last ice age.

"Cold, Cold Heart" one more time!

Never invite the glaciers over ever, ever again.

Cold, Dry, and Dusty: Still Not Everyone's Idea of an Ice Age

Is this the guy from page 35?

Sure is.

You think he'd start looking first.

You'd think so, wouldn't you?

Even during the period when glaciers covered the land, it was not often cold and wet, like a nasty winter storm. Now scientists realize that during ice ages so much water gets locked up in ice that the weather is cold, dry, and dusty. Because it was so dry, more and more land became grassland. Grass can survive in dry weather better than most forests can. Land in what is now the Great Plains changed from forests to grass. Animals that ate grass had more and more of it to munch on. Dryness changed the landscape much more than ice did.

During the coldest periods of the ice age, ice locked up so much of the seas that there was a lot more dry land all over the world. The coastlines of North America, from Maine to Florida and from California to Washington State, were much farther out than they are now. In some places, the New York coast was almost

I think I'll start looking first.

100 miles farther out. Long Island wasn't an island during the ice age but was part of what is now New York and Connecticut.

The barrier islands along the Carolinas weren't islands, either; they were joined to the mainland. The newly created Bering Sea dried up because so much seawater was frozen into ice. This meant the Beringia Bridge was exposed and the superhighway to and from North America was once again open for business. Ice-age mammals searching for food moved very freely back and forth.

Mammoths Arrive Dressed for Success

Mammoths arrived in North America at two different times via the Siberian express to the Beringia Bridge. The ancestral mammoth, ancestor of most American mammoths, came over about 1.5 million years ago. The woolly mammoth crossed only about 100,000 years ago. The woolly mammoth had a long coat of hair just perfect for surviving alongside the edges of glaciers.

Mammoths had long legs and a lot of fat on their bodies. Herds of mammoths could walk great distances in search of grassland. Mammoth bones have been found in almost every state of what would eventually become the continental United States.

While the mastodons pretty much stuck to

forests, the mammoths ate grass — a lot of it! Each one probably devoured about 400 pounds of food a day and drank more than 40 gallons of water. Mammoths had curved tusks that grew to be as

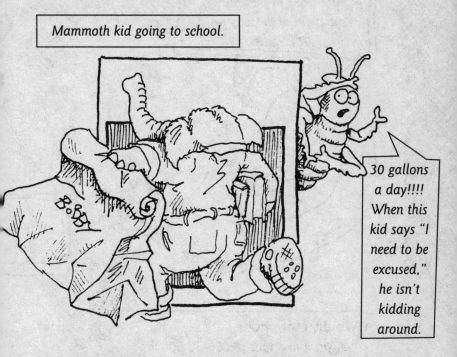

Mammoth kid going to school.

30 gallons a day!!!! When this kid says "I need to be excused," he isn't kidding around.

long as 13 feet and weighed about 185 pounds each. They used their tusks for knocking down trees, digging water holes, and to protect themselves from enemies like the saber-toothed cat.

There were many different types of mammoths. They even came in different colors. Mammoth hides have been found with black, brown, reddish-brown, and yellow hair growing from them. The Columbia mammoth had very little

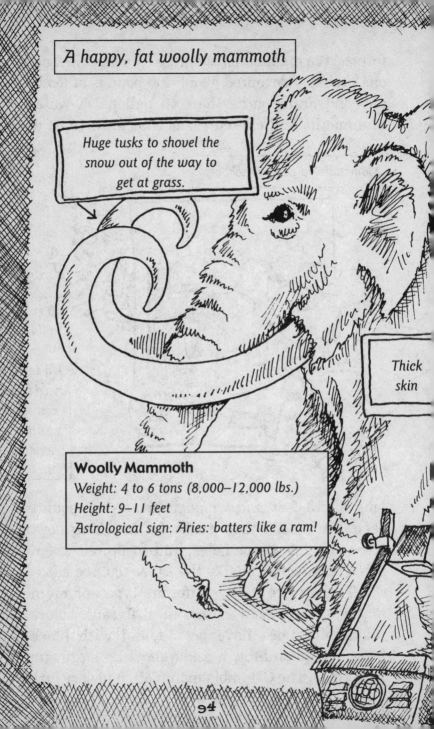

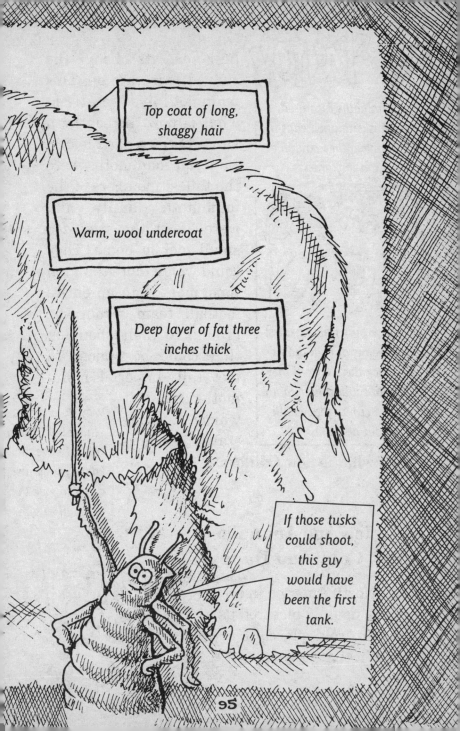

Top coat of long, shaggy hair

Warm, wool undercoat

Deep layer of fat three inches thick

If those tusks could shoot, this guy would have been the first tank.

FACT OR FICTION

Mammoths also used their tusks to open cans of chili when they couldn't find any grass.

Of course that's fiction! First of all, cans of chili didn't exist back then. Even if they did, how could a mammoth hold the can in place without a thumb?

hair on its body (he shaved twice a day). This mammoth lived mostly in what is now the southern United States and Mexico. Imperial mammoths were the tallest members of the mammoth family and were about the size of a small mobile home. They could weigh more than ten tons, more than an entire football team. From the ground to their shoulder, they could be almost 18 feet tall. Imperial mammoths liked it warm so they stayed in places like what is now California.

Why do we even talk about the play?!!! We all know you're just going to give the ball to him.

Ice-Age Animals: Fat, Cold, and Happy!

North America in an ice age is usually pictured as a barren, cold place. It wasn't that way at

How to Thaw a Mammoth (Very Carefully!)

Occasionally parts of a mammoth have been found frozen solid, including pieces of their flesh and woolly coats. In 1999, the *whole* body of a male woolly mammoth was found in Siberia. Scientists brought him up in a block of ice. As this book went to press, they began thawing out their woolly find. Guess what scientific tool they'll use to melt the ice block? A hair dryer! O.K., maybe a dozen hair dryers. They're the best tools for the job. The mammoth has to be thawed carefully to save as much of his soft parts as possible so that they can be studied. Some scientists are wondering if they can use the prehistoric animal's DNA to clone a mammoth and implant its egg in an elephant. One science lab has said that if there's DNA, no problem. Others in the scientific community think it can't be done.

In Siberia, where the whole mammoth was found iced under in the tundra, people call these frozen animals *mammut,* or "creature that lives under the earth." The word *mammoth* comes from this Russian word. According to Siberian legend, mammoths were ancient animals that lived underground like trolls and died if they came out into sunlight. The legend wasn't true. When mammoths were alive, they lived in the sunlight and ate grass all day. Don't you wonder how rumors get started?

Regardless of how cute you think they are, it's always such a bother when suffering from garden mammoths.

Mammoth Site in Hot Springs, South Dakota, has one of the largest collection of mammoth bones found in the Americas. But because mammoths lived all over what is now the United States, chances are that your own area's museum of natural history also has mammoth bones that you can look at.

all. The glaciers moved slowly. There was a lot of grass to eat. Mammals did just fine in the ice age.

Most mammals had fur made up of two types of hairs, one for insulation and the other called guard hairs for protecting the insulating fur. Fur allowed animals like saber-toothed cats to hunt in the winter.

Colder winters meant bigger and bigger animals. Not just the mammoth, but many animals were huge. Why did animals grow so

Unfortunately, I don't have any fur, so I spent most of the ice age in front of my stove.

One of the best places to see the remains of North America's ice-age mammals is right in the middle of downtown Los Angeles at the **La Brea Tar Pits.** There, giant imperial mammoths and other animals mistook the tar for water and got stuck. Then predators like the saber-toothed cats and dire wolves attacked the stuck animals and got stuck themselves. The remains in the La Brea Tar Pits are amazingly well preserved. On a walking tour of the pits and the **George C. Page Museum,** you can see the fossils and life-size models that move and make noises to show how these mammals lived. Despite a chain-link fence, the occasional stray pigeon or squirrel still gets stuck in the pits, which, in a word, is . . . the *pits*!

As if this situation isn't bad enough already, is that you making those bubbles?

OK. Here's ten more good reasons I didn't get out much during the ice age.

large? Large animals lose body heat at a slower rate than smaller animals do, so it's better to be big in the cold. In fact, the United States had some of the largest mammals the world has ever seen.

Top Ten
American Ice-Age Mammals

1. **Beavers** were the size of black bears and had teeth the size of bayonets. Prehistoric beavers could cut down a tree in minutes.

2. **Giant ground sloths** were as big as elephants. They could eat leaves from trees two stories tall. Think of Jabba the Hutt with teeth and fur.

3. **Prehistoric bears** were bigger and could run faster than today's grizzly bears.

4. **Saber-toothed cats** had extra-thick fur so they didn't have to store fat and could stay sleek hunters. They could hunt year-round and slice open bellies with their razor-sharp front teeth.

5. **Rats** were the size of baby cows.

6. **Prehistoric camels** managed just fine in North America during the ice age. They walked ahead of the glaciers and lived in American deserts.

7. **Bison** stood seven feet tall at the hump and had horns that measured six feet from tip to tip.

8. **American woolly mammoths** were about 14 feet tall, with 10-foot-long curved tusks. They stored fat from summer feasts under their woolly coats.

9. **Woolly rhinoceroses** had an extra-thick coat as well as an extra layer of fat to keep them warm, just like the woolly mammoth.

10. **Giant mastodons** roamed freely from California to the New York island.

Want to see what the next ice age might look like? You can see glaciers in North America today. Just remember that they can be dangerous, and it's best to go with a guide.

Glacier National Park in Montana

Mount McKinley National Park in Alaska

Mount Rainier National Park in Washington State

Olympic National Park in Washington State

Yosemite National Park in California

Is Another Ice Age Coming?

Some scientists believe that we are in between glaciers today. Because the glaciers seem to come and go, some scientists believe the next ice age could begin as early as 2014. It's possible that humans have changed the environment so much that we won't have another ice age. But it's also possible that the long-range forecast over the next 20,000 years calls for another ice age. So if you like to ski or snowboard, maybe you're in for a treat. Stay tuned to the weather channel for details. And remember: Eat up, it's better to be fat and happy when it gets cold!

I'll be honest with you, I thought the ice age was going to be a lot worse. Sure, there was plenty of snow and ice in Canada, but there's almost always a lot of snow and ice in Canada! How do you think they got so good at hockey? I guess there was some pretty thick ice in New York and Chicago, too, but for the animals that

lived in California at the time, the "ice age"
was more like the "nice age" if you ask me.
I'll admit the Great Lakes are pretty cool,
and the woolly mammoth makes me laugh
because he looks like an elephant with a
bad perm, but I can't help but think we
were still missing somebody in this era.
You guessed it . . . humans.

Chapter 5

We're Here . . . Because We're Here

You may have noticed that no humans are listed on the Top Ten American Ice-Age Mammals. That's because most scientists believe that North and South America were two of the last stops on *Homo sapiens sapiens*' world tour and that they didn't get here until the ice age was almost over.

To find out where humans came from, most scientists say you have to take a quick trip to Africa. There, scientists have discovered several

TIME LINE

3.1 million years ago
In Africa, "Lucy," a four-foot-tall hominid, walks on two feet

200,000 years ago to 40,000 years ago
Two hominid species, the Neanderthals and *Homo sapiens sapiens*, spread across the Earth

45,000 to 30,000 years ago
The Neanderthals die out, and *Homo sapiens sapiens* is the only hominid species left

106

ancient primate species called hominids who lived on the edge of the grassland and walked on two feet at least 3.1 million years ago. One of the first hominid skeletons found is called "Lucy." The scientists who discovered her were so excited they played the Beatles' song "Lucy in the Sky with Diamonds" all night long and named the skeleton Lucy.

You guys! You so got me! I'm totally surprised! You're the best friend a 3.1-million-year-old skeleton ever had!

?? to 12,500 years ago
People like you and me arrive in America; lots of arguments about exactly when

11,000 to 6,000 years ago
End of last ice age. All the mammoths and other big ice-age mammals mysteriously die

Also 11,000 to 6,000 years ago
Small ice-age mammals throw a party celebrating disappearance of big ice-age mammals

By about one million years ago, hominids did more than walk around on two feet. Sadly, however, they hadn't learned to make shoes yet. They had learned to make tools, though. They also learned to use fire. At least two of the hominid species, the Neanderthals and *Homo sapiens*

Hello. I'm a Homo sapiens sapiens.

Is there an echo in here?

sapiens, moved out of Africa to Europe and the Middle East.

Neanderthals in America?

Between 40,000 and 35,000 years ago, a dramatic change happened. The Neanderthals died out and a species that scientists call *Homo sapiens sapiens* (like New York, New York: so nice they named it twice) was the only hominid species left. Most scientists believe that the Neanderthals died out before any of them came to North America. However, Dr. Louis Leakey, who found the first evidence of humans in Africa, visited California in 1962. He thought it was possible that Neanderthals might have lived in the California Mojave Desert as long as 100,000 years ago. So far, most scientists don't believe the evidence supports Dr. Leakey's findings, but remember: The experts have been wrong before. It wasn't so long ago that experts thought the sun moved around the Earth.

That Old Herd Instinct

By about 30,000 years ago, modern humans, the species *Homo sapiens sapiens*, had spread to nearly all parts of the world. The big mystery is when they finally made it to the Americas. Until very recently, most scientists believed that people came to North America from Siberia over the frozen Beringia Bridge about 12,000 years ago. If humans did cross Beringia, they probably followed herds of animals. People often follow herds of animals, chasing lunch or because animals

At the **Calico Early Man Archaeological Site** in Yerma, California, there are mostly just rocks, but if that's what you like, then it's well worth the tour.

show them the best routes to get from one place to another. (Daniel Boone followed a bison trail to hack out the Wilderness Road in Tennessee.)

I sure hope those guys are trick-or-treating, because if they're seriously trying to fool anybody, this is embarrassing.

Beringia during the ice age doesn't sound like a great place for a vacation, does it? Yet it was. Warm winds from the Pacific kept Beringia free of ice most of the year, so it was dotted with freshwater lakes and ponds. The huge herds of grazing animals would have been easy for the humans to see and follow. These animals would have led people to lakes, ponds, rivers, salt licks, and better yet, to dinner. Humans could eat many of the same plants that animals ate. They could also eat the animals if they could kill them, and these early Americans were hunters as well as plant eaters. In fact, they could eat almost anything — except brussels sprouts. No one can eat brussels sprouts!

Liz, sweetie, you can think anything you like about brussel sprouts, but you're writing a book here. We're going to get letters!

Yeah, Liz, back off.

Yoo-hoo!
Look Where We Are!!

In the 1990s, scientists were able to prove that humans lived on Monte Verde, Chile, at least 12,500 years ago. Archaeologists have found some of the earliest houses in either of the Americas at the very tip of South America. These shelters are made of animal bones covered by animal hides. Some minute bits of carbon from a fire might even be 30,000 years old. These new discoveries rocked the world of prehistoric human history. If humans had just arrived in North America over Beringia, how did these ancient people get all the way to Chile so quickly? I mean, even if they had bicycles — which they didn't — just imagine how long this trip would take!

The Dating Game

Paleontologists, geologists, archaeologists, and other scientists share more than just confusing names that are hard to pronounce. They also share information. Part of their job is to accurately date what they've found and there are more and more tools and techniques that help them do this. For example, argon-argon dating may sound like two creatures from another planet going to a movie, but it's actually a way to date fossils too old for radiocarbon dating. Radiocarbon dating is the most well-known technique, but it only works for relatively recent prehistoric history like the ice age, about 100,000 years ago.

In 1949, while studying the atom bomb, Dr. Willard Libby discovered that radiocarbon 14, because it decays at a steady rate, can be used to accurately date bones and charcoal from the past. Since then, there have been constant new discoveries that make radiocarbon dating and other dating techniques more and more accurate. Still, there's plenty of room for mistakes and plenty of room for arguments.

However People Got Here, They Stayed ... and They Ate a Lot!

A team of American and Chilean archaeologists worked for two decades on the Monte Verde site in Chile, trying to figure out how people got there. From the study of poop and of bones, scientists have discovered that the people of Monte Verde gathered berries in the spring, chestnuts in the fall, and also ate mushrooms and marsh grasses. They hunted small game. Sometimes they went down to the Pacific Ocean, 30 miles away, for shellfish. (That's a long way to go for lobster!) The settlement on Monte Verde means that humans arrived in the Americas much earlier than most scientists previously thought.

There are lots of other hints that humans may have been in the Americas longer than 12,000 years. Human artifacts from the Meadowcroft Rockshelter site in Pennsylvania may be more than 20,000 years old. Other sites in South America and California may be even older.

I can eat for days just on what's smeared on your average three-year-old's T-shirt.

Whoever these humans were and wherever they came from, they quickly spread out over North America. A human being is not a small mammal. There are more than 4,000 mammals alive today, and only two or three hundred of them are larger than we are. And we're not just big in size: We make a big impact on our surroundings, and we have big appetites, too. For many of the animals already living here, this became a disaster.

One thing archaeologists know about these new arrivals is that they were highly skilled at making beautiful stone tools. Their brains were exactly the same size as yours; if you went back in time, you'd have no trouble fitting in. (But with no TV and no ice cream, what's the point?)

Besides stone, these first-comers also made tools out of bones and deer antlers, and used animal skins for clothes so they could live in the

Oh, yeah! It's really warm, but next time I'm definitely removing the tusks.

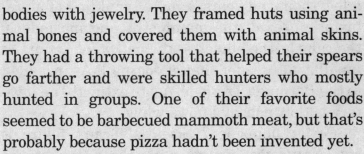

I'm going to hit water this time for sure!

cold. They made spear points and needles, and decorated their tools and adorned their bodies with jewelry. They framed huts using animal bones and covered them with animal skins. They had a throwing tool that helped their spears go farther and were skilled hunters who mostly hunted in groups. One of their favorite foods seemed to be barbecued mammoth meat, but that's probably because pizza hadn't been invented yet.

The glaciers from the most recent ice age began to retreat about 18,000 to 20,000 years ago. It started to turn warm again in North America, just as it had several times over the past million years. The ice that formed the Beringia Bridge melted. Water flowed back into the sea, and the Beringia Bridge flooded. The glaciers that covered most of North America thawed, and all the water that had been locked up in ice began to melt. From California to the Carolinas, the growing oceans flooded the coastal areas. Now the humans and ice-age mammals of North America were locked together in a new, warm land.

Uh-oh!

The Great Whodunit? Why Did Millions of Giant Mammals Die?

When the first humans arrived in the Americas, the lands teemed with horses, camels, rhinoceroses, mammoths, and mastodons. In just a few thousand years, a mere twinkling of a prehistoric eye, all the mammoths and mastodons, the camels, the horses — they all went kaput. As in: all gone, deader than a doornail! As in: sailed to the Bermuda Triangle. As in: extinct! The mystery is that nobody knows why.

What happened? Scientists can't figure it out. Naturally, just as with the death of the

Sorry, guys, you have to be gigantic!

Daniel, Daniel, Daniel, buddy, c'mon. Aliens? You're thinking aliens? Leave it to an artist. It's like the chicken and egg thing. Does thinking weird make a person an artist? Or does being an artist make a person think weird?

Artist's Concept (Possible Explanation)

dinosaurs and other prehistoric mysteries, there are lots of theories.

Too warm! Too cold!

Ice ages don't end all at once. Sometimes it gets a lot colder in one place as it is getting warmer in another (sort of like when your little brother or sister pees in the swimming pool). In North America at the end of the ice age, the summers got cooler just at the same time the winters got warmer. According to this theory, the large mammals couldn't adapt to the cooler summers.

Too dry!

When the world warmed up, the ice caps melted, drowning the Beringia Bridge. You'd think all that melting ice would mean a lot of freshwater, but most of the glacier ice flowed back into the sea. Some scientists believe there wasn't enough freshwater for the animals left on land. There was also much less snowfall or rainfall, and the large ice-age mammals needed huge amounts of freshwater to survive. Together, three woolly mammoths could drain a large-size pond all at once. That's probably about ten million glasses of water, not to mention a whole bunch of trips to the bathroom!

The problem with all these theories is that the ice-age mammals had already survived many, many changes of weather. Why would they only have died once humans were on the scene?

They're studying my what??? Ohh, that's soooo disgusting! I'm so embarrassed! As if killing me wasn't enough!

That's the big question. Scientists have recently found poop or dung from extinct mammoths and other ice-age animals in caves in Nevada and Arizona. They are hoping that by studying the DNA from the poop, they will find out exactly how the animals died. DNA is the part of a cell that contains the clues to each living creature's exact nature.

These days, many scientists believe that what wiped out the ice-age mammals is staring us in the face. Go look in the mirror. One of your ice-age ancestors probably didn't look all that different from you, and those ancestors could be the guilty party!

Scientists believe that there were probably only a half million to a million people in the Americas when the mammoths died out. So how could fewer than a million people, just a little more than the population of Vermont, have caused the death of *all* the mammoths and so many other mammals such as the horse and giant ground sloth? It seems impossible, yet computer studies show that it is possible that a relatively small number of human hunters could have killed enough animals so that many species would become extinct. Remember, you don't have to kill off *all* the animals to gradually make it impossible for them to mate and have babies. (That's why we now have an "endangered species" list, so we can try to prevent future extinctions!)

Animals in Asia and Europe had a long time to get used to humans and to learn to fear them. The animals in North America had no experience

OK, Grok. You run up and sneeze in his face! Don't worry, Krag and I are right behind you. And we both have sticks!

with humans. And humans also carry germs. Perhaps even the horses and camels in the Americas died because they couldn't fight off germs carried by the humans who had recently arrived from Asia. Nearly 10,000 years later, when Europeans arrived in North America, the same thing happened to the people already living here. Many of them couldn't fight off the germs the Europeans brought.

The Ice Age Cometh, the Ice Age Goeth — Now What?

After the mammoth and ice-age mammals died, humans weren't alone on the continent.

Top Ten Extinct American Ice-Age Mammals

1. The horse — *EXTINCT*

2. The camel — *EXTINCT*

3. Imperial mammoth — *EXTINCT*

4. Woolly mammoth — *EXTINCT**

   (*Although on a tiny island off Siberia, some mammoths survived until 4,000 years ago.)

5. Woolly rhinoceros — *EXTINCT*

6. Giant mastodon — *EXTINCT*

They had lots of company. There were millions of bison, deer, antelope, rabbits, prairie dogs, bears, wolves, birds, and other animals. Most of the smaller mammal species survived. And don't forget the zillions of bugs. That's right, *zillions*! Makes your skin crawl just thinking about it. One of those bugs would find a home in the houses and temples that the humans were building. Yup, it had six hairy legs and those two little hairs on its butt. The humans would go on to many, many wacky adventures. They would find awesome, horrible, and wacky ways to live in every corner of North America (and the cockroach was always nearby!).

7. Giant ground sloth — **EXTINCT**

8. Giant bison with eight-foot horns — **EXTINCT**

9. Saber-toothed cats — **EXTINCT**

10. Dire wolves — **EXTINCT**

I wish everybody

would quit talking about those little hairs on my butt! I've survived five extinctions, and all anyone can talk about is those darn hairs. (I'd gladly shave them off, but then I wouldn't know if something was sneaking up behind me, and I might not survive to see the next extinction.)

Anyway, time sure flies when you're trying not to get stepped on by a woolly mammoth! Now that humans have begun to show up, things are getting even more exciting, aren't they? (I haven't met this "Lucy" person, but anybody who can keep scientists up all night partying must be pretty special.)

Personally though, I get the feeling the ice-age

mammals might not have let humans follow them to North America if they knew people would turn around and use them for food, clothing, and even shelter. Some thanks they got, huh? You humans owe us!

But then you guys learned to grow your own

food and build stuff out of wood and clay. In our next book, Liz and I will tell you all about how people went about making North America their home. I'm talking about the awesome ancient Americans. From spear-wielding hunters to pyramid-building Maya, you'll see how humans became the most amazing species on Earth. Of course, that's only if you don't count cockroaches.

Bye-bye for now!

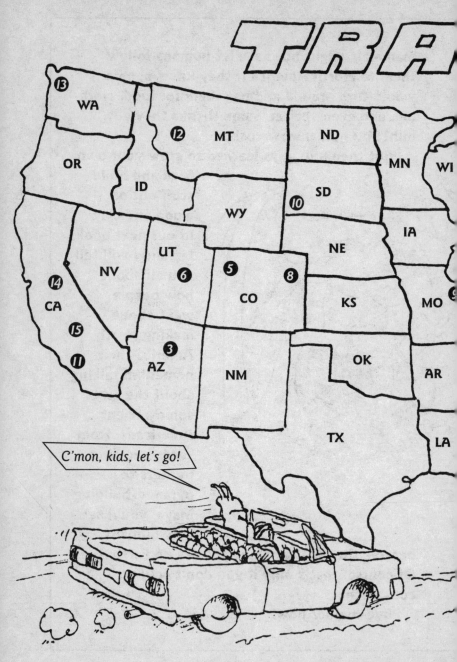

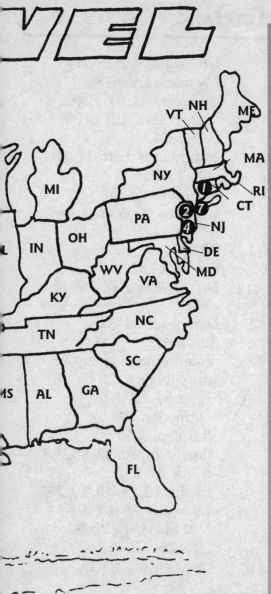

Index

dogs, 77, 90

E

Eobasilius, 64
extinction, 21, 44–59,
  117–120
  Cretaceous, 47
  Devonian, 46
  K-T, 47
  mammalian, 116–121
  Ordovician, 46
  Permian, 46
  theories, 48–52
  Triassic, 46–47

F

flowers, 32
fossils, 18–20, 30, 44

G

gastroliths, 23
geologists, 21
geomorphologists, 21
geophysicists, 21
giant ground sloths,
  101, 121
glaciers, 87–89, 103, 115
grass, 71–74, 91
Great Lakes, 89

H

hadrosaurs, 35–37
Hadrosaurus foulkii,
  37, 43
Hendrickson, Ellen, 28

Hesperocyon, 77
Homo sapiens sapiens,
  106–111
horns, 64–65
horses, 65–66, 80, 90,
  116, 120
human beings,
  106–111, 113–115,
  118–120

I

ice age, 9, 81, 84–92, 96,
  98, 101, 103, 115, 117
insects, 32–33, 58–59, 121
iridium, 53

K

"kill curve," 56–57, 119

L

La Brea Tar Pits, 76, 99
Leakey, Louis, 108–109
Libby, Walter, 112
"Lucy," 107

M

mammals, 48, 64, 114
  extinction of, 116–121
  grass-eating, 73–74
  ice-age, 101–102
  large, 64–67, 98, 101, 117
  small, 15, 58–59, 62
mammoths, 78, 81, 90,
  92–93, 96, 97, 116,
  117–120

mammoths *(continued)*
  imperial, 96, 99, 120
  woolly, 94–95, 102,
    117, 120
mastodons, 78–81, 102,
  116, 120
meteor, 44–59
Monte Verde, Chile,
  111, 113
mountain goats, 80

N
Neanderthals, 108–109
Nivaravus, 75
nuclear winter, 57

O
oxen, 80

P
paleontologists, 20,
  22–23, 31
Pangaea, 10, 14, 15, 16,
  18, 21, 30
plants, 21, 32, 62–63,
  71–74, 91
plates, 17, 70–71, 85–86
prairie dogs, 121
primates, 68–70
pterosaurs, 45

R
rabbits, 121
radiocarbon dating, 112

rats, 101
reptiles, 29, 31, 37
rhinoceroses, 90, 102,
  116, 120
Rocky Mountains, 30,
  63, 89

S
sauropods, 22–23
Sauroposeidon, 22
Smilodon, 75–76
Stegosaurus, 24, 43

T
temperature, 51–52, 56,
  70–71, 84, 86, 117–118
Tenontosaurus, 29
Tertiary Period, 46
time lines, 14–15,
  44–45, 62–63, 84–85,
  106–107
tools, 114
travel adventures, 18,
  34, 41, 45, 70, 79, 98,
  99, 102, 109, 122–123
Tyrannosaurus rex,
  25–27, 28, 38, 43, 66

U
Ultrasaurus, 22–23, 43

V
volcanoes, 51, 63